Motels

American Retro

Unanimous

Motels

American Retro

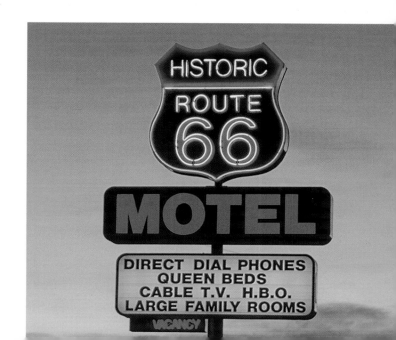

Travel strengthens America.

U. S. Travel Bureau

Contents

Introduction

"On that road the nation is steadily traveling beyond the troubles of this century, constantly heading toward finer tomorrows. The American Road is paved with hope."

1951 Ford ad

The great highways of America were its very heart and soul. They spanned the limits of this vast country from top to bottom and east to west. They carried the new breed of motorists from good to bad, from boom to bust, through towns with such names as Mammoth Cave, Kentucky; Pleasantville, New York; and Broken Bow, Nebraska; many of them with nothing more than a Main Street and a drugstore.

Along the way these arteries offered succor in the form of welcoming diners, serving plates of wholesome freshly prepared dishes—food that spawned a universal language in the shape of hot dogs, hamburgers, fries, and malts. Comfortable motels with warm rooms offered the latest in modern conveniences, from power showers to the combination television and radio set, and provided a safe haven for the night. They were clean and affordable family businesses, which allowed the nuclear family, for the first time, to explore the wonders of their own land.

Parked outside were the trappings of prosperity—Cadillacs, T-Birds, Chevrolets, and Corvettes—cars that any sane person has always wanted to drive. These were elongated giants, explosions of chrome grilles and wire wheels, creating fantasies of speed and escapism with features taken from aircraft designs and space travel. These were the only beasts capable of taming this extraordinary country, and are as representative of the United States of America as the Statue of Liberty or the Stars and Stripes.

The names of those great roads—Highway 61, Route 66, Pacific 1—have since passed into popular mythology. For those with a passion for adventure, the names evoke images of *Easy Rider*, and the lyrics of Bob Dylan and the Rolling Stones. At the same time, they are able to convey that air of safety and innocence, when mom and pop ushered the kids into the back of the family automobile and headed off on vacation.

Now this golden age is all but gone, although remnants do remain. The highways have fallen into disrepair, superseded by freeways with no recognizable character. Many diners have served their last "special," and a large number of "ma and pa" motels have been swallowed up into chains with such alluring names as Comfort Inn and Motel 6 (we are never told what happened to Motels 1 through 5). Small towns, with the whole of life encapsulated on Main Street, are a far cry from the soulless shopping malls of today. And the cars—oh those glorious, gas-guzzling monsters—have been replaced by sensible, compact, economical models with dull, dull names.

As a tribute to the post-war period when people had money in their pockets and a hankering to spend it, the four titles in the *American Retro* series draw on images, both retro and modern, that resonate with the spirit of '50s America. These pictures are paired with advertising slogans, popular sayings, puns, and quotations from personalities that bring to life an age when being economical with the truth came naturally to the advertisers and salesmen of the day, who were desperate to paint a dazzling and futuristic world in which everyone could share. Motels shamelessly claimed to offer comfort fit for the "Queen of Sheba"; car manufacturers used such buzz words as "Rocket Ride" and "Glamorous new Futuramics"; and diners bedecked themselves in chrome detailing and neon lights.

The *American Retro* series recaptures a little of what made those times so special, with images that will fill those who lived through that age with nostalgia and gently amuse and inform those who did not. Read, remember, and enjoy.

Where summer
stays and the
nation plays.

When they suggested we
stay at the Wigwam Motel,

I had my reservations.

Wigwam Motel,
Holbrook, Arizona

Route 66 is for people who will always be suckers for neon lights

(and home-cooked meals).

Hitch your wagon to a star.

Ralph Waldo Emerson

Wagon Wheel Motel,

Cuba, Missouri

OREGON TRAIL
MOTEL
6 BLKS E. OF 2ND STOP LIGHT
SGL $17⁹⁵
DBL $22⁹⁵ & UP

Sensible Rates - Air Conditioned
Phones - Color TV TRUCK PARKING PLUG IN

6 BLK. E. OF MAIN ON 26

Go west, young man, go west!

John Babsome Lane Soule

Sign for the Oregon Trail Motel,

Torrington, Wyoming 21

Oh for a lodge in some vast wilderness,

Some boundless contiguity of shade,

Where rumor of oppression and deceit,

Of unsuccessful or successful war,

Might never reach me more!

William Cowper

Frontier Motel, Cheyenne, Wyoming

ON HIGHW
ROUTE U. S. 30

CHEYENNE
WYOMING

Ranger
MOTEL

Postcard from

the Ranger Motel,

Cheyenne, Wyoming

I have a dream that one day this nation will rise up, live out the true meaning of its creed: we hold these truths to be self-evident, that all men are equal.

Martin Luther King

Lorraine Motel,
Memphis, Tennessee

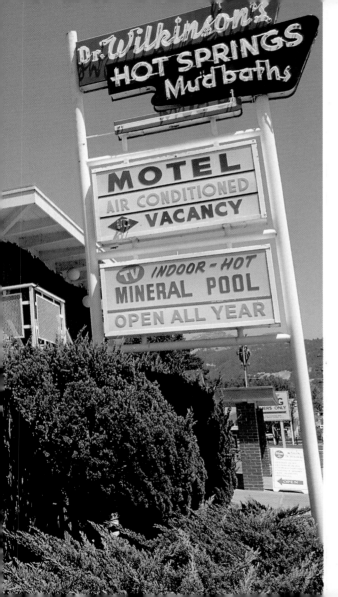

With two outdoor warm mineral water pools, and an indoor hydrojet pool open to all guests, Dr. Wilkinson's offers a true spa experience.

Dr. Wilkinson's Hot Springs Motel, Calistoga, California

30

Where summer spends the winter.

Flamingo Inn, Key West, Florida

Marry in haste; repent in Vegas.

Wedding chapel, Las Vegas, Nevada

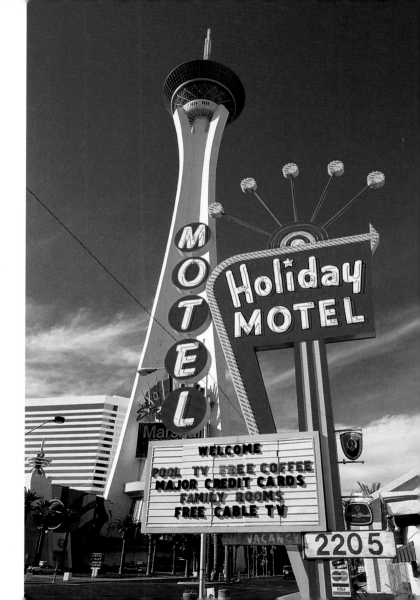

Escape from the ordinary.

A place by the sea.

Bon-Aire on the Sea, Miami Beach, Florida

Well, I find that a change of nuisances

is as good as a vacation.

David Lloyd George

Yankee hospitality.

Cold Spring Motel,

Plymouth, Massachusetts   41

43

Oh my America!

my new-found-land.

John Donne

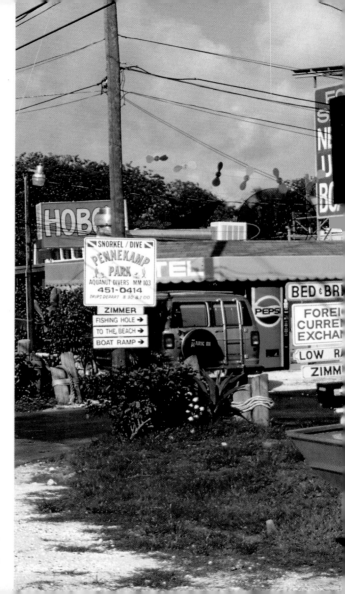

Kelly's Motel,
Key Largo, Florida

Never judge

a summer resort

by its postcards.

Abandoned motel

near Weed, California   47

Rest your head

at the place

with the headdress.

Chief Motel, near

Joshua Tree National

Monument, California   49

Like all great travelers,

I have seen more than I remember,

and remember more than I have seen.

Benjamin Disraeli

Goose Hunting Capital of the World.

Farris Hotel, Eagle Lake, Texas

With motels,

a bad sign is a bad sign.

Weathered sign
of the Chiriaco Motel

Spend the night, not a fortune.

Motel in Pioche, Nevada

From the moment you park your car, you can begin relaxing.

Dream Inn, Daytona Beach, Florida

and are dedicated to making your spa visit a very relaxing and restful time

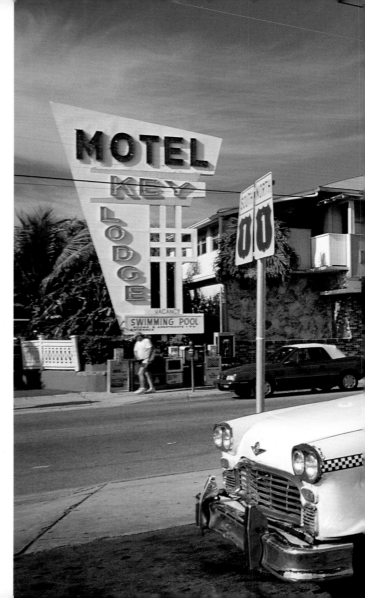

Motel in the

Florida Keys, Florida

Santa Fe

is often called

the "City Different."

You'd be surprised how much
it costs to look this cheap.

Dolly Parton

Caesar's Palace and The Mirage Hotel,

Las Vegas, Nevada

The Sunshine State.

Gulf Side Motel,
Cedar Key, Florida 73

Nature's paradise,

man's opportunity.

Hobo Inn,
Elbe, Washington 77

The lobby of some motels

is like God's waiting room.

Cold Spring Motel,

Plymouth, Massachusetts

A helluva place to lose a cow.

Ebenezer Bryce

Yeeha!

Lake View Motel, Garden City, Utah

83

True comfort

in the cradle

of the revolution.

Peg Leg Motel,

Rockport, Massachusetts

Northern exposure.

Town Motel, Gardiner, Montana

Friendly, familiar, foreign, and near.

Roxy Place Motel, Beardmore, Ontario

It is an urge, as irresistible as a tide...to travel,

and the ability to travel has forged a united country,

and reduced a vast area to the dimensions of a community.

Swan Hotel, Walt Disney World, Florida

WOODLAND MOTEL RESTAURANT

NO VACANCY

Your log cabin away from home.

They appear in early evening

and depart at the first streak of dawn,

and none knows whence or whither.

We only know that they have been.

Budget Inn, Daytona Beach, Florida

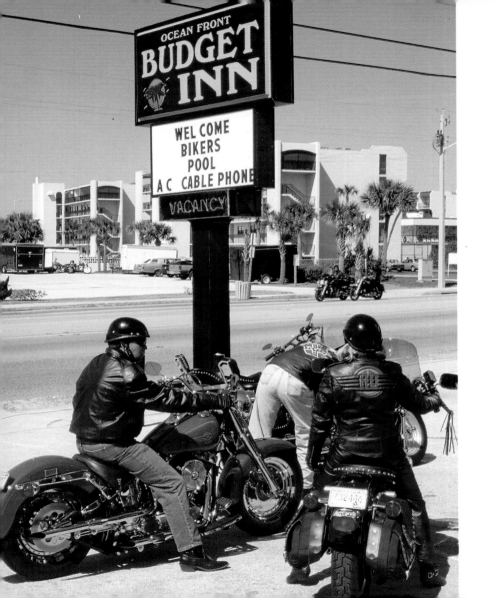

97

CASA
MOBILE
PARK

LUXURY LIVING

POOL

Smorga
Kitchen
FAMILY BUFFET

COMMERCI
40

SILVEY'S
MOTEL
VACANCY

LOW RATES
COLOR
CLEAN
AIR C
KITC

LUNCH | DINNER

OPEN
FOOD

BUDGET
MOTEL

NO VACANCY

COLOR TV
AIRCONDITIONED
LOW RATES
CLEAN & QUIET
KITCHENETTES

ATED MOVIES
WATER – REGULAR BEDS
T SPA IN ROOM

FREE
ADULT
MOVIE

Town House
MOTEL

COLOR TV · WATERBEDS · PHON
AIR COND · WEEKLY RATES ·

Crest
MOTEL

NO VACANCY

Home of the Blues,

birthplace of Rock 'n' Roll.

Lorraine Motel,

Memphis, Tennessee

Wherever you're going, you're sure to find a "B&B" to suit your needs.

MOTEL
AIR CONDITIONED
VACANCY

TV *INDOOR - HOT*
MINERAL POOL
OPEN ALL YEAR

The closest I ever got

to a life at sea

was staying in a motel

with a waterbed.

Captain's Bounty Motel,

Rockport, Massachusetts

HISTORIC
ROUTE
66

MOTEL

DIRECT DIAL PHONES
QUEEN BEDS
CABLE T.V. H.B.O.
LARGE FAMILY ROOMS

VACANCY

OK
SALOON

Cocktails

PACKAGE GOODS

TEXACO

Travel strengthens America.

Picture credits

All images reproduced by permission of Corbis Images unless otherwise stated.

Page 8/9: Motel row in Kissimmee, Florida; credit Nik Wheeler.

Page 10/11: Moonglo Motel apartments in Daytona Beach, Florida; credit Lake County Museum.

Page 12/13: Wigwam Motel on Route 66, Holbrook, Arizona; credit Nik Wheeler.

Page 14/15: Route 66 Motel sign in Kingman, Arizona; credit David Paterson.

Page 16/17: Munger Moss Motel along Route 66 in Lebanon, Missouri; reproduced by permission of Travel Ink/Walter Wolfe.

Page 18/19: Wagon Wheel Motel along Route 66 in Cuba, Missouri; reproduced by permission of Travel Ink/Walter Wolfe.

Page 20/21: Sign for the Oregon Trail Motel in Torrington, Wyoming; credit James L. Amos.

Page 22/23: Neon sign for the Frontier Motel in Cheyenne, Wyoming; credit Henry Diltz.

Page 24/25: Postcard from the Ranger Motel in Cheyenne, Wyoming; credit Lake County Museum.

Page 26/27: Lorraine Motel in Memphis, Tennessee; credit Jan Butchofsky-Houser.

Page 28/29: Dr. Wilkinson's Hot Springs Motel in Calistoga, California; credit Robert Holmes.

Page 30/31: Flamingo Inn in Key West, Florida; credit Morton Beebe.

Page 32/33: Wedding chapel in Las Vegas, Nevada; reproduced by permission Travel Ink/Simon Reddy.

Page 34/35: Stratosphere Tower Hotel and Casino in Las Vegas, Nevada; reproduced by permission Travel Ink/Simon Reddy.

Page 36/37: Bon-Aire on the Sea in Miami Beach, Florida; credit Bettmann.

Page 38/39: Dumont combination television and radio set; credit Bettmann.

Page 40/41: Cold Spring Motel in Plymouth, Massachusetts; credit Kevin Fleming.

Page 42/43: Motel on Interstate 90; credit Raymond Gehman.

Page 44/45: Kelly's Motel in Key Largo, Florida; credit Tony Arruza.

Page 46/47: Abandoned motel near Weed, California; credit Bob Rowan.

Page 48/49: Sign for the Chief Motel near Joshua Tree National Monument, California; credit Henry Diltz.

Page 50/51: Roy's Motel and Café along Route 66, California; credit Nik Wheeler.

Page 52/53: Sign on the Farris Hotel in Eagle Lake, Texas; credit Peter Johnson.

Page 54/55: Sign for the Chiriaco Motel; credit Henry Diltz.

Page 56/57: Motel in Pioche, Nevada; credit Gary Thomas Sutto.

Page 58/59: Sign for the Dream Inn in Daytona Beach, Florida; credit Tony Arruza.

Page 60/61: City Center Motel in Seattle, Washington; credit Ray Krantz.

Page 62/63: Dr. Wilkinson's Hot Springs Motel in Calistoga, California; credit Robert Holmes.

Page 64/65: Motel in the Florida Keys, Florida; reproduced by permission of Travel Ink/Abbie Enock.

Page 66/67: Loretto Motel in Santa Fe, New Mexico; credit Craig Lovell.

Page 68/69: Caesar's Palace and the Mirage Hotel in Las Vegas, Nevada; reproduced by permission of Travel Ink/Walter Wolfe.

Page 70/71: Forum of Caesar's Palace in Las Vegas, Nevada; reproduced by permission of Travel Ink/Simon Reddy.

Page 72/73: Gulf Side Motel in Cedar Key, Florida; credit Patrick Ward.

Page 74/75: Motel signs in Pigeon Forge, Tennessee; credit Galen Rowell.

Page 76/77: Hobo Inn Motel in Elbe, Washington; credit Wolfgang Kaehler.

Page 78/79: Lobby of the Cold Spring Motel in Plymouth, Massachusetts; credit Kevin Fleming.

Page 80/81: Sign for the Uranium Motel in Utah; credit Joel W. Rogers.

Page 82/83: Sign for the Lake View Café and Motel in Garden City, Utah; credit Scott T. Smith.

Page 84/85: Peg Leg Motel in Rockport, Massachusetts; credit Kevin Fleming.

Page 86/87: Gold Rush Inn in Whitehorse, Yukon Territory; credit Gunter Marx.

Page 88/89: Town Motel in Gardiner, Montana; credit Darrell Gulin.

Page 90/91: Roxy Place Motel in Beardmore, Ontario; credit Patrick Bennett.

Page 92/93: Swan Hotel in Walt Disney World, Florida; reproduced by permission Travel Ink/Abbie Enock.

Page 94/95: Sign for the Woodland Motel in Dillsboro, North Carolina; credit Owen Franken.

Page 96/97: Budget Inn in Daytona Beach, Florida; credit Patrick Ward.

Page 98/99: Motels in Sacramento, California; credit Nik Wheeler.

Page 100/101: Sign for the Lorraine Motel in Memphis, Tennessee; credit Kevin Fleming.

Page 102/103: Detail of Motel sign; credit Robert Holmes.

Page 104/105: Captain's Bounty Motel in Rockport, Massachusetts; credit Kevin Fleming.

Page 106/107: Motel along historic Route 66; credit Nik Wheeler.

Attributions

Page 8/9: Sarasota slogan, Florida State.
Page 12/13: Anon.
Page 14/15: Anon.
Page 18/19: Ralph Waldo Emerson.
Page 20/21: John Babsome Lane Soule.
Page 22/23: William Cowper.
Page 26/27: Martin Luther King.
Page 28/29: Motel promotional literature.
Page 30/31: West Palm Beach slogan, Florida State.
Page 32/33: Anon.
Page 34/35: '50s Oldsmobile ad.
Page 36/37: Anon.
Page 38/39: David Lloyd George.
Page 40/41: Motel promotional literature.
Page 44/45: John Donne.
Page 46/47: Anon.
Page 48/49: Anon.
Page 50/51: Benjamin Disraeli.
Page 52/53: Eagle Lake title.
Page 54/55: Anon.
Page 56/57: Anon.

Published by Unanimous Ltd
254–258 Goswell Road, London EC1V 7RL

A CIP catalogue record for this book is
available from the British Library.

Designer: WDA
Editor: Alison Moss
Researcher: Suzie Green

ISBN: 1 903318 19 X

Printed and bound in Spain by Bookprint, S.L, Barcelona

1 2 3 4 5 6 7 8 9